Best Start

MUSIC LESSONS
BOOK 1

for
Recorder
Fife
Flute

2nd edition

by Sarah Broughton Stalbow

First published in 2018 by Best Start Publishing

ISBN: 978-0-6485764-2-6

All musical compositions by Sarah Broughton Stalbow, except for the following by Jeremy Barnett: Lesson 4: *The Cake*, Lesson 5: *Who's the boss?*, Lesson 6: *At the Disco*, Lesson 7: *The Dance,* Lesson 8: *Mr Mouse.*

Cover art and text design by Sarah Broughton Stalbow, editing by Rob Stalbow.

A catalogue record for this book is available from the National Library of Australia

Best Start Publishing
www.beststartmusic.com

For teachers and parents

Aims

Best Start Music Lessons introduce foundational musical concepts and skills to the young beginner. As well as developing musical skills and competencies, these lessons aim to foster a love of music and music making.

Originally developed for children aged 3 to 7 years learning in a group, it is also a great resource for older students who may progress through the books faster, while still developing a strong musical foundation.

A comprehensive system of learning in which the students are truly engaged ensures that musical concepts are thoroughly understood, develops a solid foundation of key skills, and provides the best musical start possible.

Everything in this book can be played on the recorder, fife, flute, or Nuvo instruments such as the Toot.

Features include:

- Engaging and interactive - many different activities including writing, drawing, colouring, movement, improvisation.
- Slow paced progression to accomodate the youngest beginners.
- Structured lessons provide a familiar routine.
- Clear and detailed lesson plans make it easy for students to reinforce learning at home.
- Suitable for individual or group tuition.
- Activities suitable for classroom use.

Everything needed for a music lesson or home practice session is in the one book.

The skills developed in Best Start Music Lessons are readily transferable to other instruments, making the transition to new instruments and school band programs easy.

Background

Best Start Music Lessons emphasizes the development of aural and rhythmic skills.

The methodologies of **Kodaly**, **Orff** and **Dalcroze** have provided inspiration for many of the activities in this book; however, Best Start Music Lessons do not claim to embody any one or all of these methods. Inspiration has also been drawn from the works of respected author, educator and composer, **Paul Harris**, and from the wonderful piano classes at the **Australian Music Schools**, Sydney. A list of further reading is provided on the Best Start Music website: www.beststartmusic.com.

Kodaly rhythm names are used throughout, rather than western rhythmic notation names. This gives young beginners the ability to easily identify rhythmic values and patterns, and learn to sight read rhythms quickly and accurately.

Music teachers may choose to introduce western rhythmic notation names concurrently, or at a later stage.

Solfege note names are used for some singing activities to expose children to another way of naming notes and thinking about sounds.

Best Start Music Lessons aim to empower children by giving them the tools and skills to decode and analyse music easily.

How to use this book

Best Start Music Lessons can be used in a variety of ways to suit individual students and teachers.

- Older students - may spend one week on each lesson.

- Younger students and group lessons - may spend multiple weeks on each lesson.

- Teachers can choose which activities to spend more time on each week according to the flow of lessons and individual student needs.

- No need to complete all activities in one lesson before moving on to the next.

- Lessons can be repeated on multiple instruments.

- When repeating the lessons, musical skills and activities are familiar - this gives time to concentrate on tone and technique.

A good teacher is an invaluable resource!

Backing tracks are provided for each song on the Best Start Music Lessons website and YouTube Channel.

www.beststartmusic.com

Options for progression

The following chart demonstrates four different pathways a student and teacher may choose:

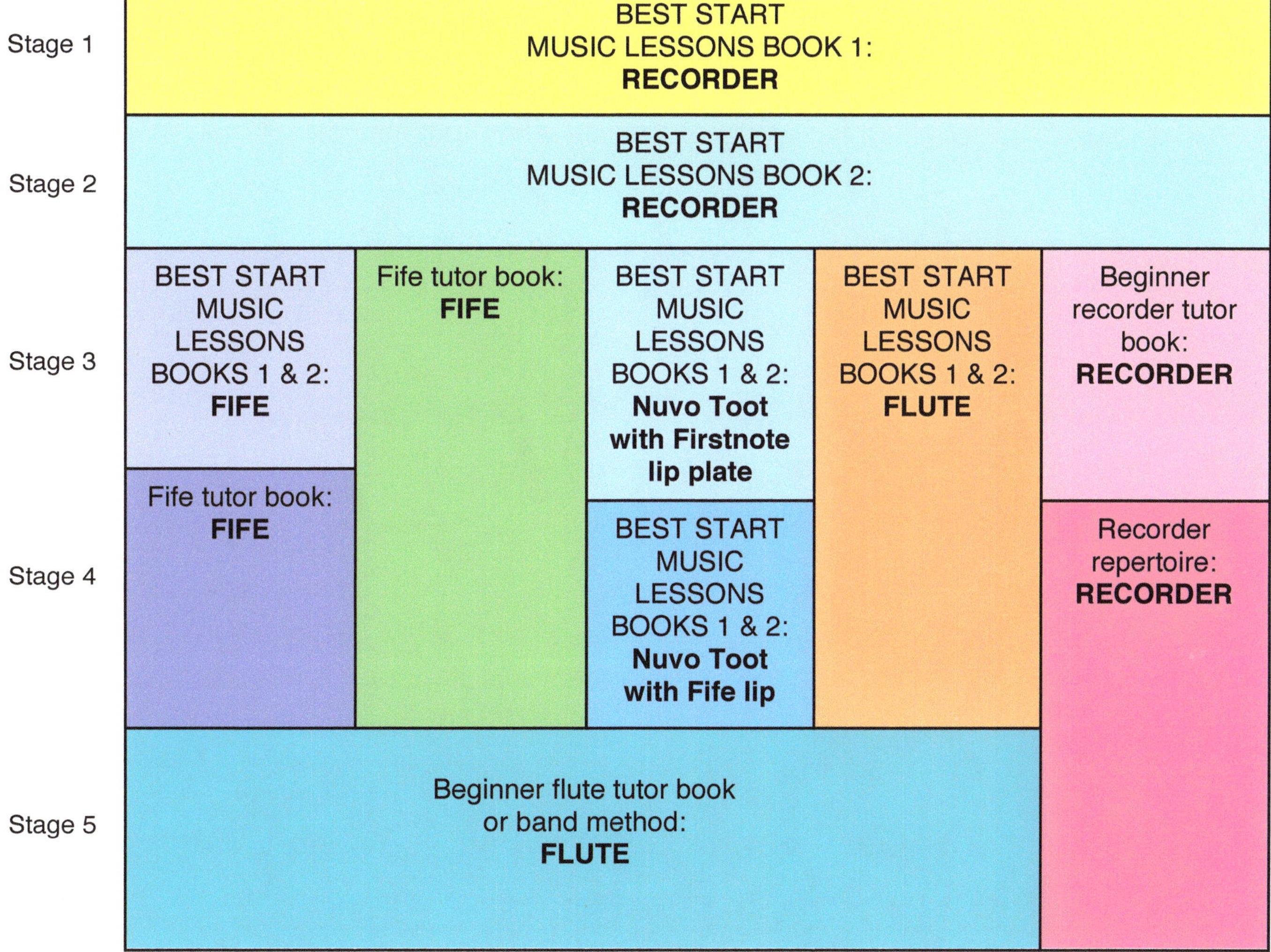

For Students

Look out for these symbols:

WRITING activities:

COLOURING activities:

Play along with the BACKING TRACK:

You will notice that there a some BALLOONS on every page, like this:

Every time you do an activity that has balloons attached to it, you can colour one balloon in. You can do the activities at home or in your lesson.

In this book you'll be learning:

* How to play an instrument

* How to read music

* How to play music in a group

* Listening skills

* How to compose music

You can find the backing tracks for all of the songs on the Best Start Music Lessons website and YouTube channel: **www.beststartmusic.com**

We really hope you enjoy them as much as we do!

Your teacher will show you how to blow your
instrument and how to clean it.

RULES FOR LESSONS

1. Always listen to your teacher.

2. Only play when your teacher says to.

3. Have a go!

4. Be positive.

STICKERS

There is a sticker chart at the back of this book. Teachers or parents can give you a sticker
for good behaviour, good listening and positive attitude.

Lesson 1

1.

Warm Up

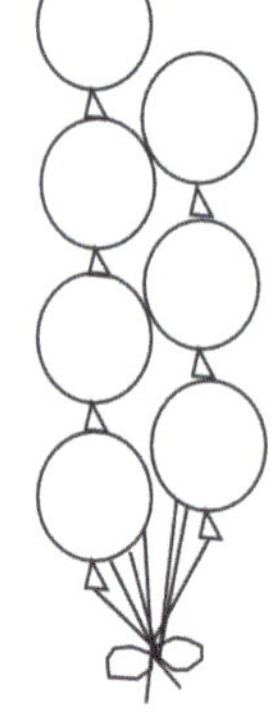

Call and response:	Music and movement:
Call and response rhythms with your teacher.	*In the Hall of the Mountain King* *by Edvard Grieg* Imagine a story - a troll lives alone in a cave in the mountain. It's night, it's dark, he's creeping through the forest surrounding his cave. He knows someone is there - but where are they? Who is it?! Get ready for a surprise at the end!!
Use clapping and body percussion.	When the music is quiet, make your body small and clap or tap quietly.
	When the music is loud, make your movements bigger and louder!

2.

Elements of Music

Ta	Ta-a	Rest
One beat note	Two beat note	One beat silence
Clap and say:	Clap once and say:	Hands out to the side
"Ta"	"Ta-a"	Think: "Rest"

3.

Rhythm

Say the rhythm names as you clap.

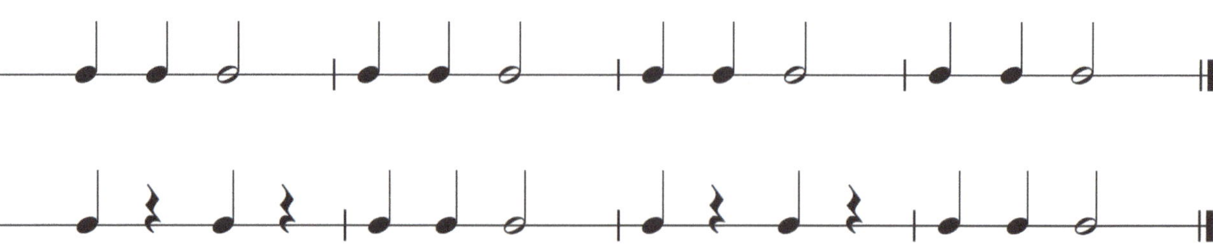

4.

New Note

B

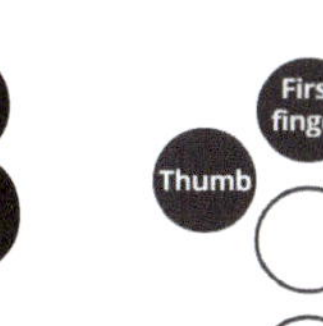

Recorder

Fife / Flute

1. Hold up your LEFT hand.

2. LEFT hand goes on top.

3. Cover the THUMB hole and the FIRST finger hole.

4. This is the note B.

5. Squeeze and check for FULL CIRCLE imprints on your fingers.

Tip: if you don't cover the entire hole, air will leak out and you won't get the right note - or you might get a squeak!

Try playing the rhythms you clapped on the opposite page using a B.

5.

Long Notes

1. Play a B for 4 counts.

Blow a steady, even air stream.

No bumps in the sound!

2. Sing a B - listen to the pitch of the note.

3. Play B again - listen.

Do the sounds match?

Tip: If you are playing the recorder, blow GENTLY…

6.

Compose

Improvise!

Make up a short song called:

"The Mouse Creeps and Steals the Cheese"

You can use any sounds you want to tell a musical story, including clapping, stamping and the note B.

Turn over the page for more!

7.

In music the note B is written on the middle line, like this:

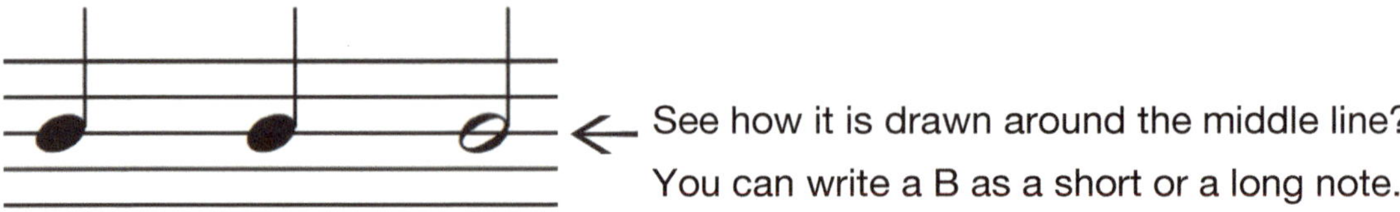

← See how it is drawn around the middle line?

You can write a B as a short or a long note.

8.

Clap Sing Play

First: clap the rhythm.
Next: sing the note names.
Then: play it!

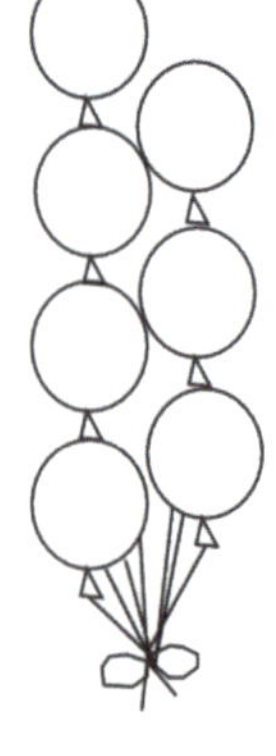

Twinkle Star

Twinkle twinkle little star

How I wonder what you are

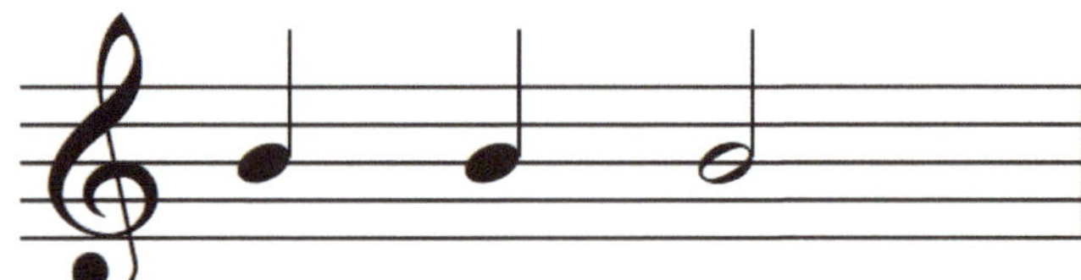

Up above the world so high,
Like a diamond in the sky,
Twinkle twinkle little star

Supplementary material

Clap then play these rhythms on their own, or as duets.

You could also play these on percussion instruments.

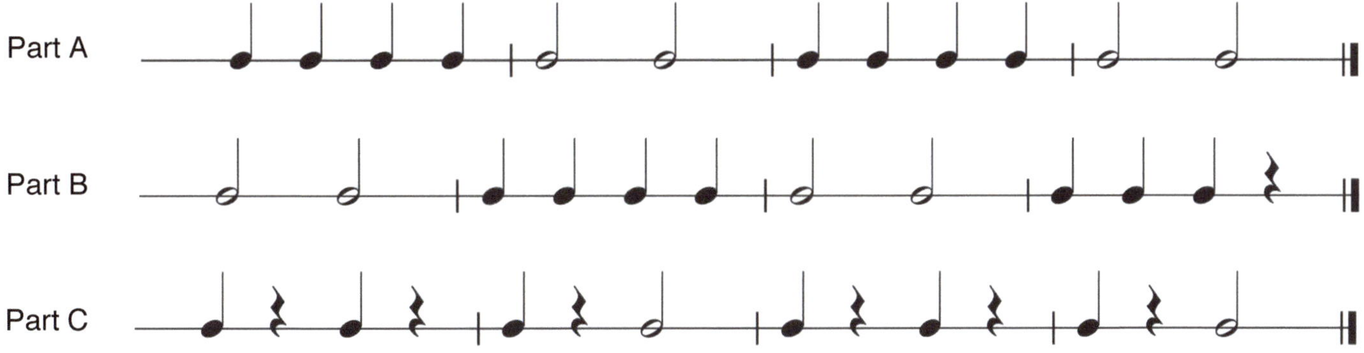

Draw a Ta

Draw a Ta-a

Draw a rest

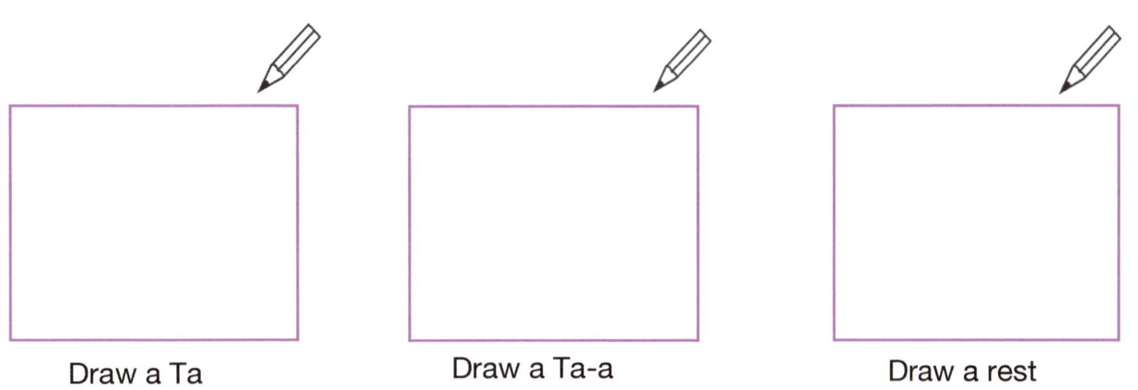

See how the note **B** is drawn around the middle line?

Draw some **B**s around the middle line

Lesson 2 ●●

1.
Warm Up

| Call and response:

Clapping and body percussion. | Music and movement:

Intermezzo from Cavalliera Rusticana

by Pietro Mascagni

Hold a soft toy, doll or pet - real or imaginary! It is late and your toy is very sleepy. Get them ready for bed with slow, gentle movements. Brush teeth, put on pyjamas, tuck into bed and gently pat to sleep with long, slow strokes. |

2.
Long Notes

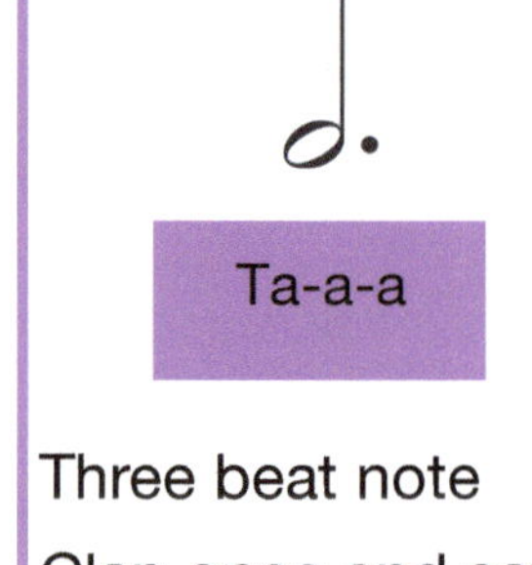

1. Hold up your LEFT hand.
2. Find a B on your instrument.
3. Play a B for 5 counts.

   Blow a steady, even air stream.

   No bumps in the sound!
4. Sing a B - listen to the pitch of the note.
5. Play B again - listen.

   Do the sounds match?

Tip: LEFT hand goes on top!

And, if you are playing the recorder, blow GENTLY…

3.
Revision

Can you name and clap each of these?

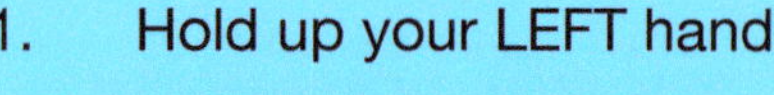

4.
Elements of Music

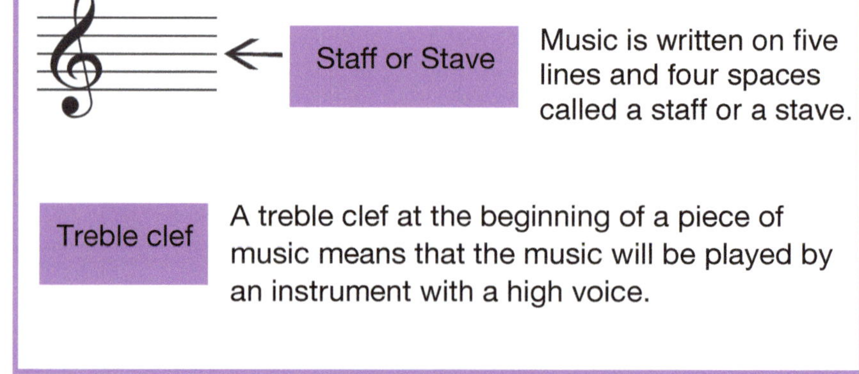

Three beat note
Clap once and say "Ta-a-a"

Music is written on five lines and four spaces called a staff or a stave.

A treble clef at the beginning of a piece of music means that the music will be played by an instrument with a high voice.

5.

Rhythm

6.

Aural

Developing inner hearing*

Divide into two groups and decide on a steady pulse.

1. Group 1 claps two beats: "1, 2"

2. Group 2 echoes, clapping two beats: "3, 4"

3. Repeat and maintain a steady pulse!

Try other variations such as:

Group 1 claps three beats and Group 2 claps the fourth beat.

*Adapted from Paul Harris, *Improve Your Teaching! Teaching Beginners: A new approach for instrumental and singing teachers* (Faber Music, 2008) 17

7.

New Song

Optional lyrics:
Creep, creep,
Trick or treat,
One, two…
I tricked you!

Trick or treat

Can you point to the treble clef?
Draw a circle around all the rests.

Turn over the page for more!

Supplementary material

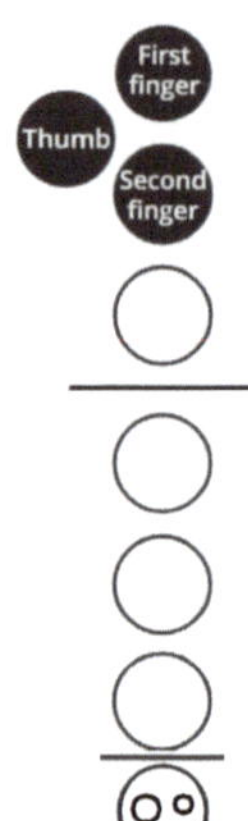

Recorder   Fife / Flute

Clap then play these rhythms using the notes A and B

Play them on their own, or as duets.

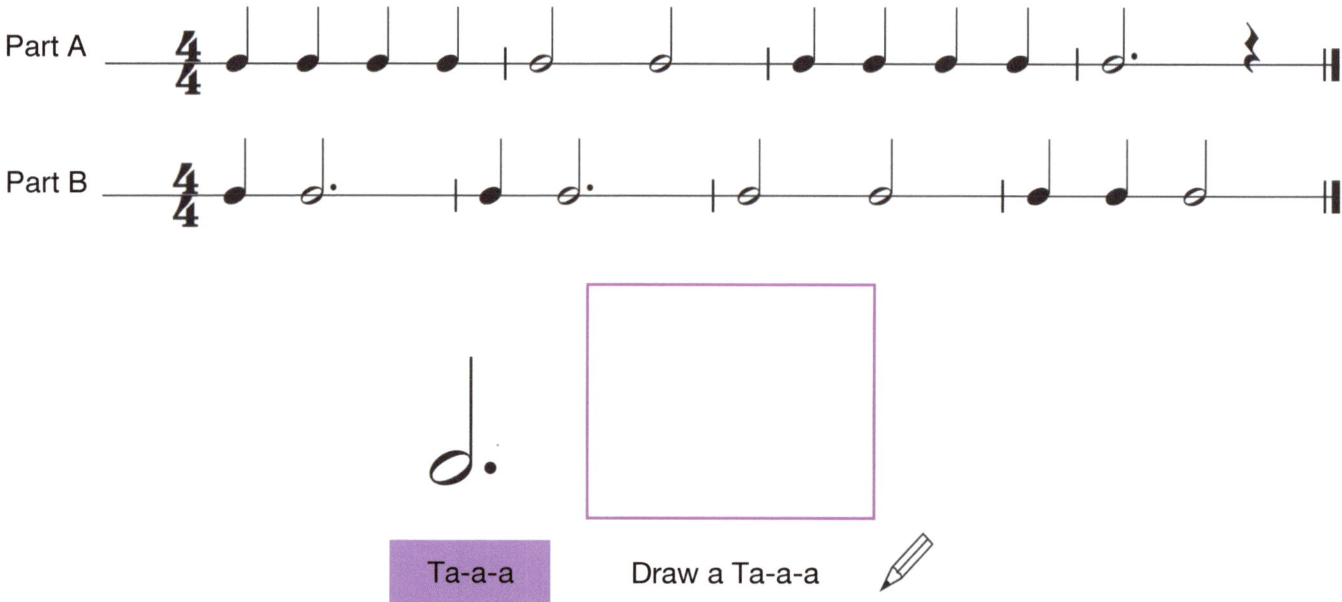

This is how to draw a treble clef. Trace over the treble clefs below,
then try drawing some on your own.

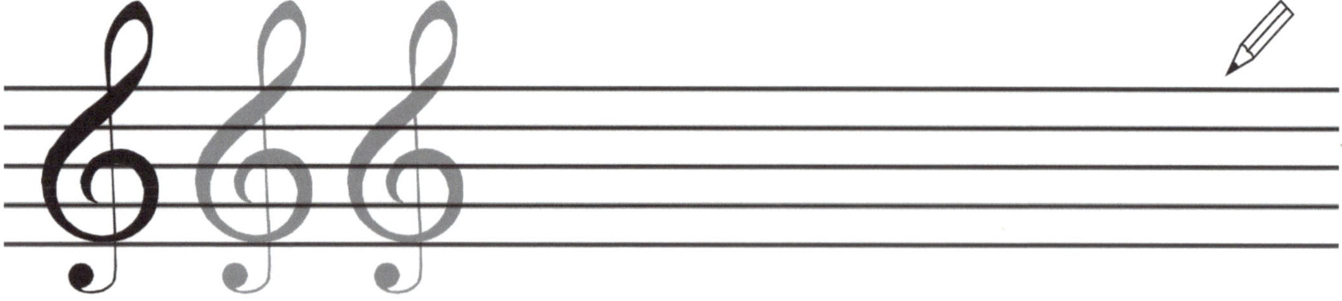

The staff (or stave) has five lines and four spaces.
Count the lines from the bottom up.
Count the spaces from the bottom up.

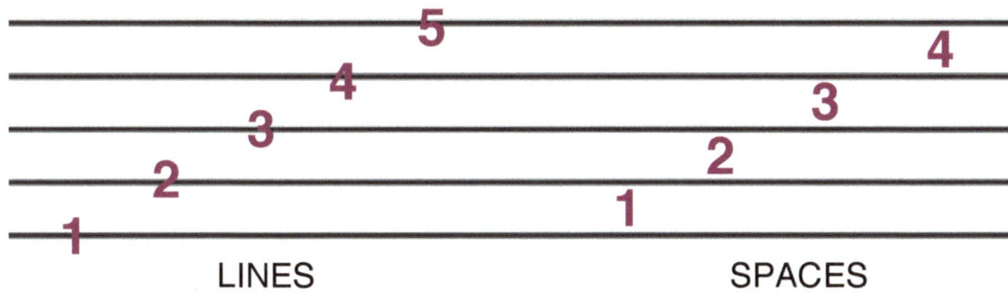

LINES   SPACES

Number the lines starting at the bottom.

Number the spaces starting at the bottom.

13

Lesson 3

1.
Warm Up

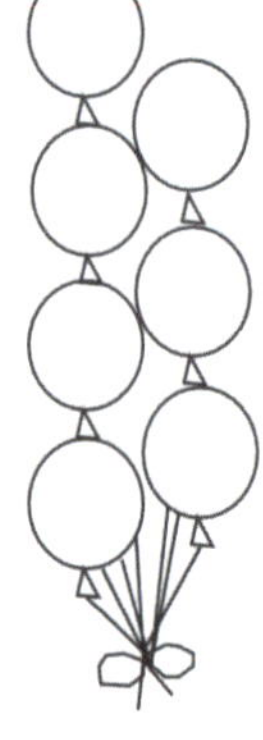

Pulse:

1. Clap, tap, or stamp a steady pulse.
2. Use different parts of your body.
3. Expression: try soft and loud, grumpy and dreamy.
4. Tell a story with the sounds.

Music and movement:

Dance of the Sugar Plum Fairy

by Pyotr Ilyich Tchaikovsky

Imagine a story: you are a mischievous fairy or an elf sneaking into your house to sprinkle magic and fairy dust.

Keep the beat with small fairy claps or tip-toes. Look over your shoulder, has someone seen you?

When the music swirls, swirl your arms to sprinkle fairy dust everywhere. Imagine your magic is making all of the furniture rise up into the air as you lift your hands up!

2.
Long Notes

1. Hold up your LEFT hand.
2. Find a B on your instrument.
3. Play a B for 6 counts.

Listen and make a beautiful sound!

Tip: LEFT hand goes on top!
And, if you are playing the recorder, blow GENTLY…

3.
Revision

Can you name each of these?

4.
Elements of Music

Music is divided up into BARS by BARLINES: A DOUBLE BARLINE
shows the end of a song.

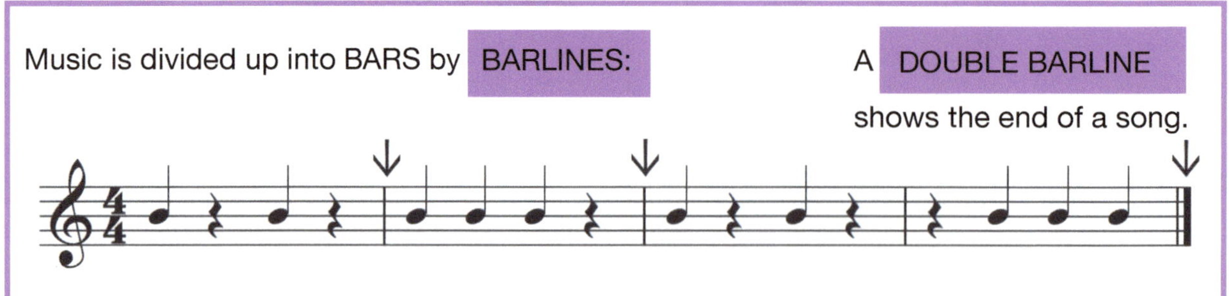

5.

A

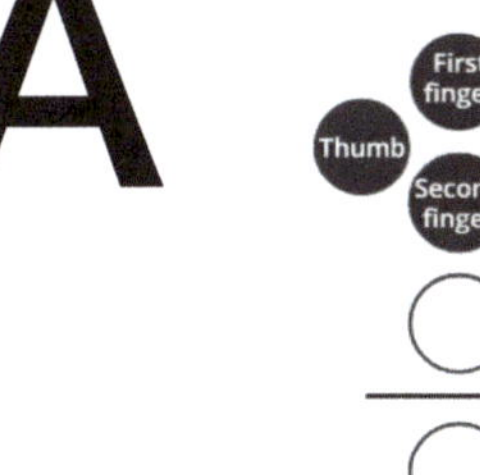

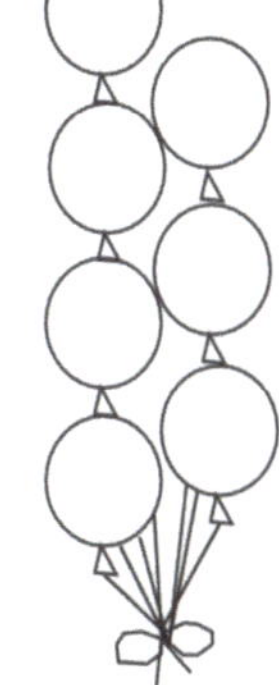

1. Hold up your LEFT hand.

2. LEFT hand goes on top.

3. Cover the THUMB hole, the FIRST finger hole, and the SECOND finger hole.

4. This is the note A.

5. Squeeze and check for FULL CIRCLE imprints on your fingers.

Play an A for 6 counts. Sing an A, listen and play again.

Wiggles!

While you blow a long A, lift your finger up and down to wobble between A and B.

6.

Clap and say the rhythm names.

Then play using the note A.

Point to the DOUBLE BARLINES

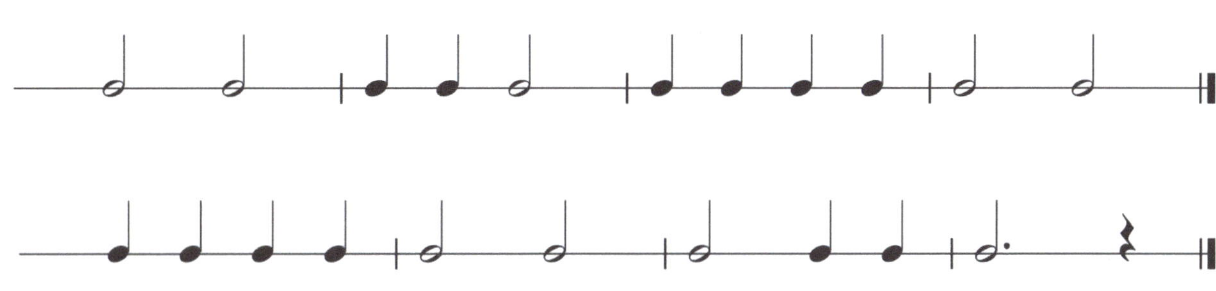

7.

Developing inner hearing*

1. Clap four beats: "1, 2, 3, 4"

2. Choose a beat to think silently.

3. Continue repeating, always being silent on your chosen beat.

To make it harder, each person choose a different beat to be silent on!

Copycats!

Listen and then sing:

Doh doh re

Re re mi

Mi mi fah

Fah fah soh

Try some more Doh Re Mi patterns!

*Adapted from Paul Harris, *Improve Your Teaching! Teaching Beginners: A new approach for instrumental and singing teachers* (Faber Music, 2008) 17

8.

In music the note A is written in the second space,
like this:

See how it is drawn inside the second space?

You can write an A as a short or a long note.

Draw some **A**s in the second space:

9.

Clap Sing Play

First: clap the rhythm.
Next: sing the note names.
Then: play it!

Optional lyrics:
Bubble bath and glitter glue,
Make this spell come true!

The Spell

Can you point to the BARLINES,

and the DOUBLE BARLINE?

10.

Improvise!

Make up a short song called:

  "The Football Game Where the Ball Burst"

You can use any sounds you want to tell a
musical story, including clapping, stamping,
clicking, squeaking, and the notes B and A.

Supplementary material

Clap then play these rhythms on their own, as duets, or as trios.

You could also play these on percussion instruments.

Part A

Part B

Part A

Part B

Part C

Lesson 4

1. Warm Up

Follow the leader:	Music and movement:
One person claps the beat, the next person joins in clapping a simple ostinato (repeating rhythmic pattern).	*William Tell Overture FInale* *by Gioachino Rossini* A horse race - listen and identify each section of the music:
One person can be the leader - everybody copies the leader's DYNAMICS and EXPRESSION.	1. Opening: pretend to play the trumpet to announce the arrival of the King, Queen and all the horses. 2. Galop in a circle, change directions when the music changes. 3. Take turns to bow to the kind and queen. 4. Galop again. 5. Jump and cheer for the end of the race!

DYNAMICS - how loud or soft the music is.

EXPRESSION - the feeling that the music expresses.

2. Long Notes

1. Hold up your LEFT hand.
2. Find a B on your instrument.
3. Play a B for 6 counts.
4. Play an A for 6 counts.

Listen and make a beautiful sound!

Remember:
LEFT hand goes on top!

wiggles! 

While you blow a long note, lift your finger up and down to wiggle between A and B. This is also known as a **trill**.

3. Tongue

When we start each note with the tip of our tongue, the notes sound clean, clear and professional!

Say:	"Too too too"
Whisper:	"Too too too"
Blow on your hand:	"Too too too"
Blow on your instrument:	"Too too too"

4.
Revision

Can you name each of these?

5.
Elements of Music

Great big whole note

Four beat note
Clap and say:
"Great Big Whole Note"

The numbers at the start of music are called the

TIME SIGNATURE

This time signature has a 4 on the top - this means that there are four beats in each bar of music.

6.
Rhythm

Clap and say the rhythm names.
Choose whether to play B or A.

Can you point to the TIME SIGNATURE?

7.
Aural

Listening: High/Low, Jumping/Stepping

Listen to some notes or a tune played on any instrument.

1. If they are HIGH notes, stand and stretch your arms up high.

2. If they are LOW notes, crouch down low.

3. If the notes step SMOOTHLY, walk very carefully and smoothly.

4. If the notes JUMP from low to high (or high to low), jump up and down!

Copycats!
Listen and then sing:

Try some more Doh Re Mi patterns!

Turn over the page for more!

8.

Clap Sing Play

First: clap the rhythm.
Next: sing the note names.
Then: play it!

Mixing mixing bake,
Icing icing cake,
Decorate,
Don't be late,
For some cake!

The Cake 

Can you point to the DOUBLE BAR LINE?

What does it mean?

9.

See how you can draw a Great Big Whole Note around a line or in a space?

Hint:

B goes around the middle line.

A sits in the second space.

Can you point to which one is B?

Which one is A?

Draw some Great Big Whole Notes around the lines and in the spaces.

Supplementary material

Clap then play these rhythms on their own, as duets, or as trios.

You could also play these on percussion instruments.

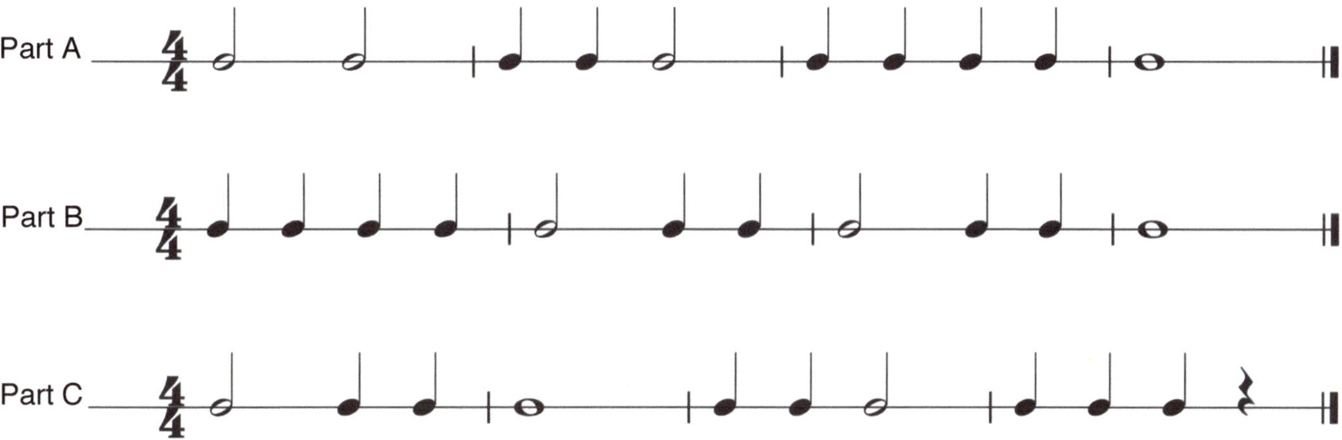

Go back and play a song from one of the previous lessons.

Solos

Pick one of the songs you have learned and perform it as a solo for your class, your family, pets or toys!

Lesson 5

1. Warm Up

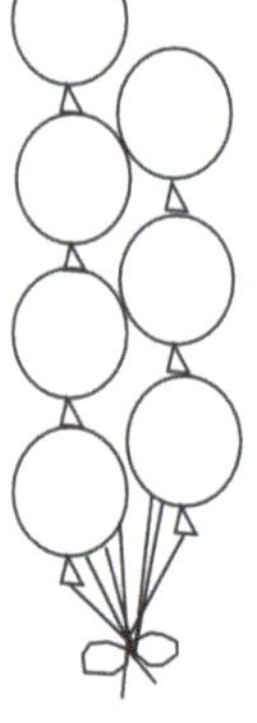

Partner clapping game:

1. Clap your hands 4 times.
2. Clap hands with your partner 4 times.
3. Repeat.

Make it harder:

1. 2 claps + 2 partner claps.
2. 1 clap + 1 partner clap.
3. Repeat!

Music and movement:

Hedwig's Theme: Prologue from Harry Potter and the Sorcerer's Stone

by John Williams

Imagine you are an owl and a wizard has given you a magical letter to deliver. Flap your wings in time with the music.

As the music swirls up high, swoop your arms up above your head.

Watch out for wolves trying to steal the letter!

When the music changes, imagine you have landed on a branch - scurry along a branch or windowsill in time with the music while still flapping your wings.

2. Long Notes

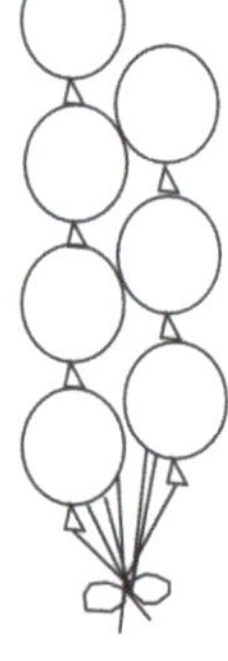

1. Hold up your LEFT hand.
2. Find a B on your instrument.
3. Play a B for 7 counts.
4. Play an A for 7 counts.

Listen and make a beautiful sound!

Remember:
LEFT hand goes on top!

wiggles! 

While you blow a long note, lift your finger up and down to wiggle between A and B.

3. Revision

Can you name and clap each of these?

4.

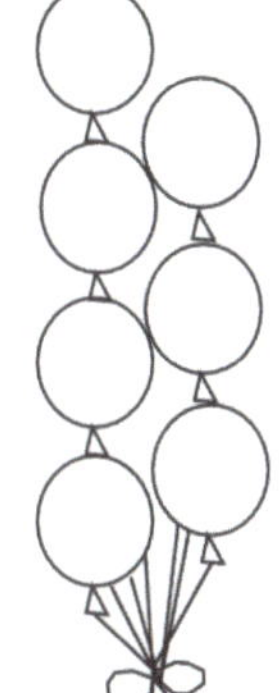

When we start each note with the tip of our tongue, the notes sound clean, clear and professional!

Say:	"Too too too too"
Whisper:	"Too too too too"
Blow on your hand:	"Too too too too"
Blow on your instrument:	"Too too too too"

5.

New Note

G

Recorder

Fife / Flute

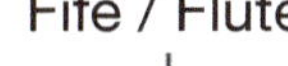

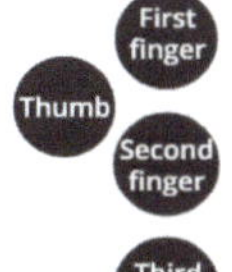

1. Hold up your LEFT hand.

2. LEFT hand goes on top.

3. Cover the THUMB hole, the FIRST finger hole, the SECOND finger hole, and the THIRD finger hole.

4. This is the note G.

5. Squeeze and check for FULL CIRCLE imprints on your fingers.

Play a G for 7 counts.
Sing a G - listen.
Play another G.

Wiggles! 

While you blow a long note, lift your finger up and down to wobble between G and A.

Which finger moves up and down?

6.

Rhythm

Clap and say the rhythm names.

Play using the note G.

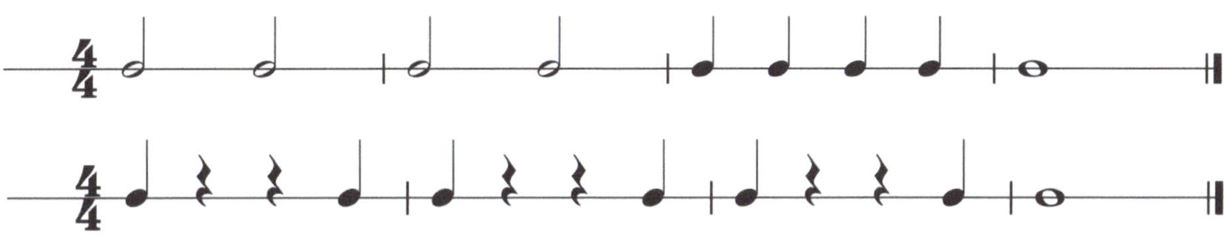

Turn over the page for more!

New Song

Clap Sing Play

First: clap the rhythm.
Next: sing the note names.
Then: play it!

How many G's can you count in this song?

How many A's are there?

Who's the boss? 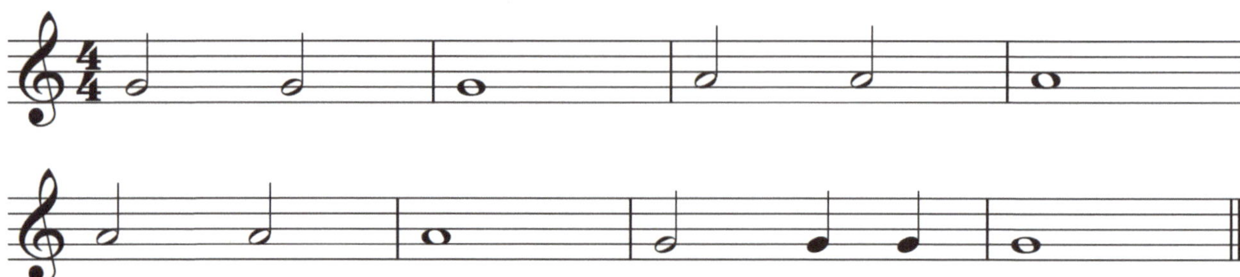

8.

Aural

Major / minor - Happy / Sad

Listen to the chords or 5 note scale played on the piano or other instrument.

If it sounds happy (Major), stand up straight with arms above your head.

If it sounds sad (minor), crouch down or touch your toes.

Copycats!

Listen and then sing:

Doh, doh re mi

Re, re mi fah

Mi fah soh

Soh soh fah

Fah fah re

Mi, mi re doh

Try some more Doh Re Mi patterns!

9.

Read / Write

In music the note G is drawn around the second line, like this:

See how it is drawn around the second line?

You can write a G as a short or a long note.

Draw some G's around the second line:

Supplementary material

Clap then play these rhythms on their own, as duets, or as a trio.

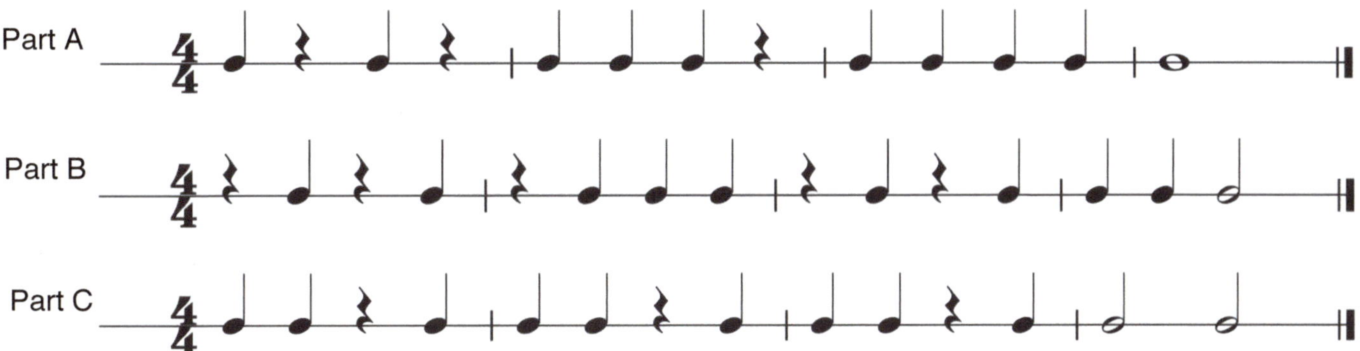

Going to the Beach 

Clap Sing Play

First: clap the rhythm.
Next: sing the note names.
Then: play it!

Go back and play some songs from the previous lessons.

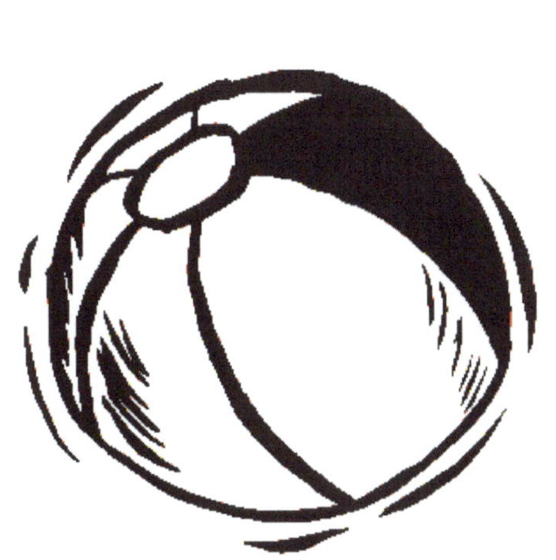

25

Lesson 6

1.

Warm Up

Call and response:	Music and movement:
Call and response rhythms with your teacher in 3/4 time! Use clapping and body percussion.	Choose one of the songs you have listened to in a previous lesson to do again: - *In the Hall of the Mountain King* - *Intermezzo from Cavalliera Rusticana* - *Dance of the Sugar Plum Fairy* - *William Tell Overture* - *Hedwig's Theme*

2.

Long Notes

1. Hold up your LEFT hand.
2. Find a B on your instrument.
3. Play a B for 8 counts.
4. Play an A for 8 counts.
5. Play a G for 8 counts.

Listen and make a beautiful sound!

Remember:
LEFT hand goes on top!

wiggles! 

While you blow a long note, lift your finger up and down to change between A and B.

Now change between G and A.

3.

Revision

Can you name each of these?

4.

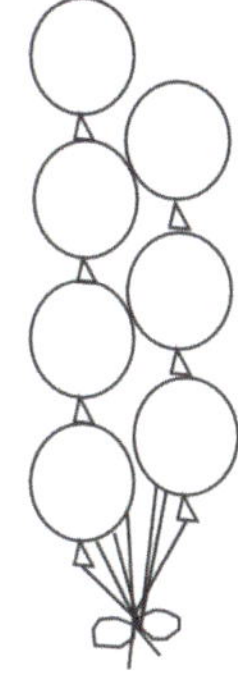

Start each note with the tip of your tongue.

Say:	"Too too too too too"
Whisper:	"Too too too too too"
Blow on your hand:	"Too too too too too"
Blow on your instrument:	"Too too too too too"

5.

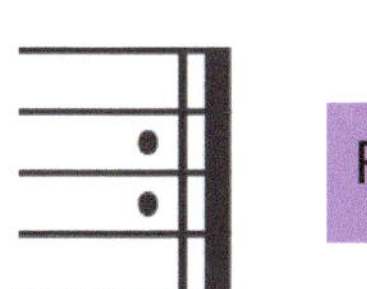

Two dots next to a double barline make a REAPEAT SIGN.

This means play it again!

6.

Clap and say the rhythm names.
Choose which note to play.

Draw two dots next to the double bar lines to make REPEAT SIGNS.

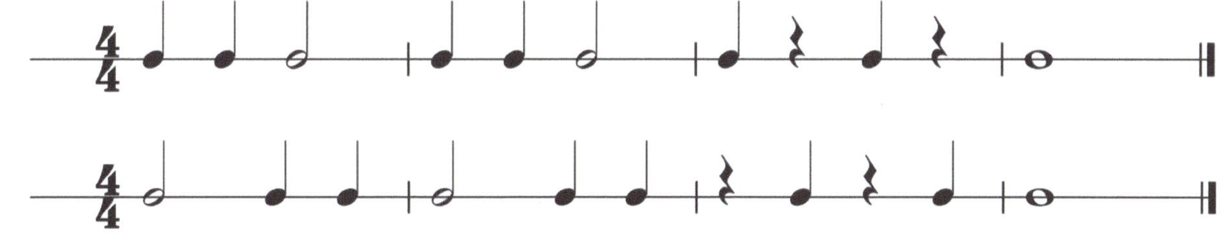

7.

Improvise!

Make up a short song called:

"The Ballerina and the Monster"

You can use any sounds or notes to tell a musical story.

8.

Clap Sing Play

First: clap the rhythm.
Next: sing the note names.
Then: play it!

Can you point to the TIME SIGNATURE?

What does a number 4 on the top mean?

At the Disco 

9.

Triple or Duple?

Swaying music has 3 beats in each bar (triple).

Marching music has 2 beats in each bar (duple).

1. Listen to the music.

2. Is the beat in groups of 3 or 2?

   Is it swaying music or marching music?

3. Sway or march in time with the music!

Copycats!

Listen and then sing:

   Doh re mi

   Re mi fah

   Mi fah soh

   Soh, fah mi re

   Doh re mi fah soh

   Soh fah mi re doh

Try some more Doh Re Mi patterns!

Supplementary material

Clap then play these rhythms on their own, as duets, or as a trio.

Hide and Seek

Draw a B around the
MIDDLE LINE.

Draw an A inside the
SECOND SPACE.

Draw a G around the
SECOND LINE.

Go back and play some songs
from the previous lessons.

Lesson 7

1.

Warm Up

Follow the leader:	Music and movement:
One person claps the beat, the next person joins in clapping a simple ostinato (repeating rhythmic pattern).	*O Fortuna, Fortuna Iperatrix Mundi* *from Carmina Burana by Carl Orff*
	Listen for the singers: Ta Ta Ta Ta.
	Listen for the instruments in the background: Ti-ti, Ti-ti, Ti-ti, Ti-ti.
	Listen for loud and soft.
One person can be the leader - everybody copies the leader's DYNAMICS and EXPRESSION.	Imagine you are building a huge castle. Hammer the bricks down: Ta Ta Ta Ta.
	Use your fingers to scurry like mice: Ti-ti, Ti-ti, Ti-ti, Ti-ti.

2.

Long Notes

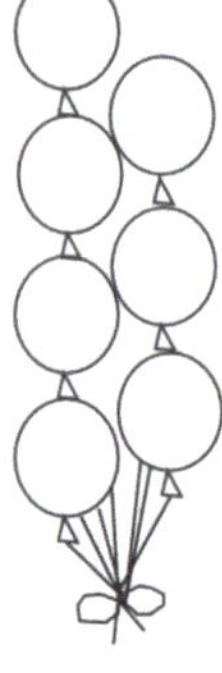

1. Hold up your LEFT hand.
2. Find a B on your instrument.
3. Play a B for 9 counts.
4. Play an A for 9 counts.
5. Play a G for 9 counts.

Listen and make a beautiful sound!

Listen carefully to your sound - is it beautiful and smooth, like honey dripping off a spoon?!

wiggles! 

While you blow a long note, lift your finger up and down to change between A and B.

Now change between G and A.

3.

Revision

Can you name each of these?

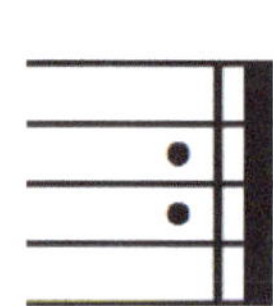

4.

Start every note with the tip of your tongue.

Say:	"Too too too too too"
Whisper:	"Too too too too too"
Blow on your hand:	"Too too too too too"
Blow on your instrument:	"Too too too too too"

Can you tongue short and spiky notes?
This is called STACCATO.

Can you tongue long, smooth notes? This is called LEGATO.

5.

Ti-ti

(tee-tee)

One beat pattern - two notes in one beat

Clap on the first one and say "Ti-ti"

Draw a Ti-ti

This TIME SIGNATURE has a three on the top.

This means that there are three beats in each bar of music.

6.

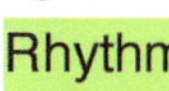

Clap and say the rhythm names.

Choose which note to play.

Can you point to the REPEAT signs and the TIME SIGNATURE?

7.

Compose

8.

New Song

Can you point to the TIME SIGNATURE?

What does a number 3 on the top mean?

The Dance 

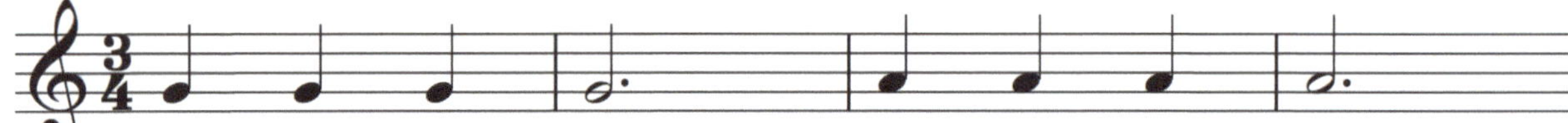

9.

Aural

Major / minor - Happy / Sad

Listen to the chords or 5 note scale played on the piano or other instrument.

If it sounds happy (Major), stand up straight with arms above your head.

If it sounds sad (minor), crouch down or touch your toes.

Copycats!

Listen and then sing:

Doh re mi

Re mi fah

Mi fah soh

Soh, fah mi re

Soh fah mi re doh

Try some more Doh Re Mi patterns!

Supplementary material

Clap then play these rhythms on their own, as duets, or as a trio.

Dressing Up 

Point to a B - B goes around the middle line.

Notice the STEM can go DOWN as well as UP for B.

Dressing up in a costume,
Dressing up in a crown.
Dressing up as a monster,
Dressing up time is now!

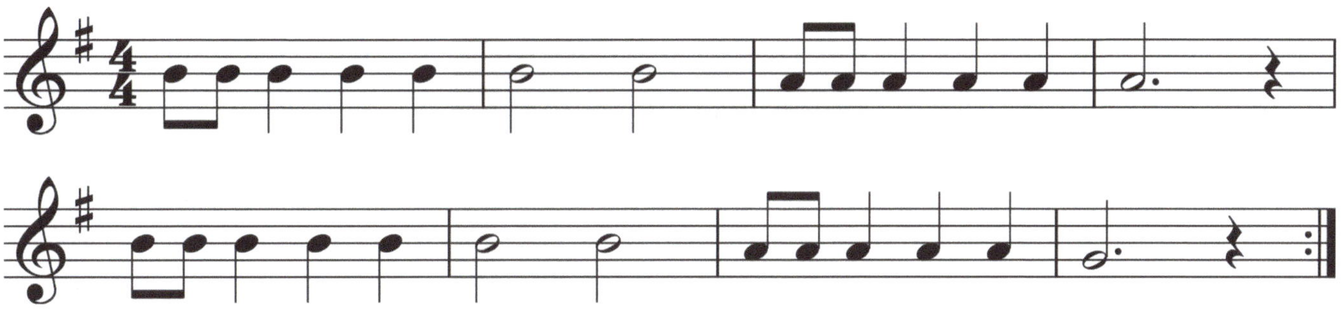

Go back and play some songs from the previous lessons.

Solos

Pick one of the songs you have learned and perform it as a solo for your class, your family, pets, or your toys!

Lesson 8

1. Warm Up

Feet and Hands:

1. Keep the beat with your feet: **Ta Ta Ta Ta**

2. Clap one **Ti-ti**

Keep your feet going!

When you can do one Tee-tee, try clapping two or more in a row!

Music and movement:

Swan Theme from Swan Lake

by Pyotr Ilyich Tchaikovsky

Dynamics - we use Italian words to describe how loud or soft music is.

Forte - this means loud

Mezzo forte - moderately loud

Piano - soft

Listen to the music - sit when it is soft, kneel when it is mezzo forte and stand when it is forte! You can also flap your arms gracefully like the wings of a swan.

2. Long Notes

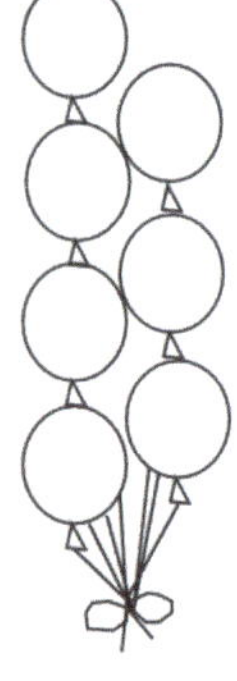

1. Hold up your LEFT hand.
2. Find a B on your instrument.
3. Play a B for 10 counts.
4. Play an A for 10 counts.
5. Play a G for 10 counts.

Listen carefully to your sound - is it smooth and beautiful?

While you blow a long note, lift your finger up and down to change between A and B.

Now change between G and A.

3. Revision

These Great Big Whole Notes are written around lines or in a space.

Which one is B? Which one is A? Which one is G?

4.

Tongue

Start every note with the tip of your tongue.

Say:	"Too too too too"
Whisper:	"Too too too too"
Blow on your hand:	"Too too too too"
Blow on your instrument:	"Too too too too"

How many notes can you tongue clearly in one breath?

Write your answer here:

5.

Rhythm

Clap and say the rhythm names.

Choose which note to play.

6.

New Song

Clap Sing Play

First: clap the rhythm
Next: sing the note names
Then: play it!

Super snail, super snail,
Go, go!
Super snail, super snail,
Not slow!

Super Snail

How many **B**s are in this song?
How many **A**s?

What do the two dots at the end mean?

7.

Triple or Duple?

Swaying music has 3 beats in each bar (triple).

Marching music has 2 beats in each bar (duple).

1. Listen to the music.

2. Is the beat in groups of 3 or 2?

   Is it swaying music or marching music?

3. Sway or march in time with the music!

Copycats!

Listen and then sing:

   Doh re mi

   Re mi fah

   Mi fah soh

   Soh lah soh

   Soh fah mi re doh

Try some more Doh Re Mi patterns!

8.

Improvise!

Make up a short song called:

"Climbing a Tree"

You can use any sounds or notes to tell a musical story.

Think about patterns of notes that climb higher, and patterns of notes that climb down lower.

9.

Look at the line of music below.

See how you can draw a Ta around a line or in a space?

Count and write your answer:

How many **B**s? ______________

How many **A**s? ______________

How many **G**s? ______________

Hint:

B goes around the middle line.

A sits in the second space.

G goes around the second line.

Supplementary material

Clap then play these rhythms on their own, as duets, or as a trio.

Mister Mouse

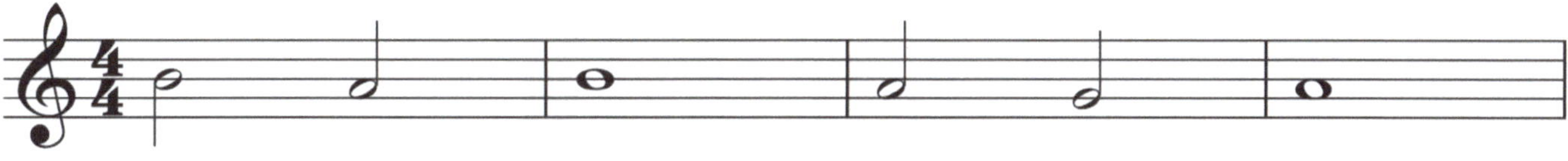

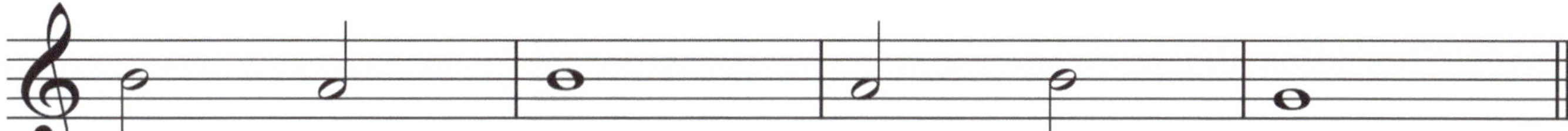

Solos

Pick one of the songs
you have learned and
perform it as a solo for
your class, your family,
pets, or your toys!

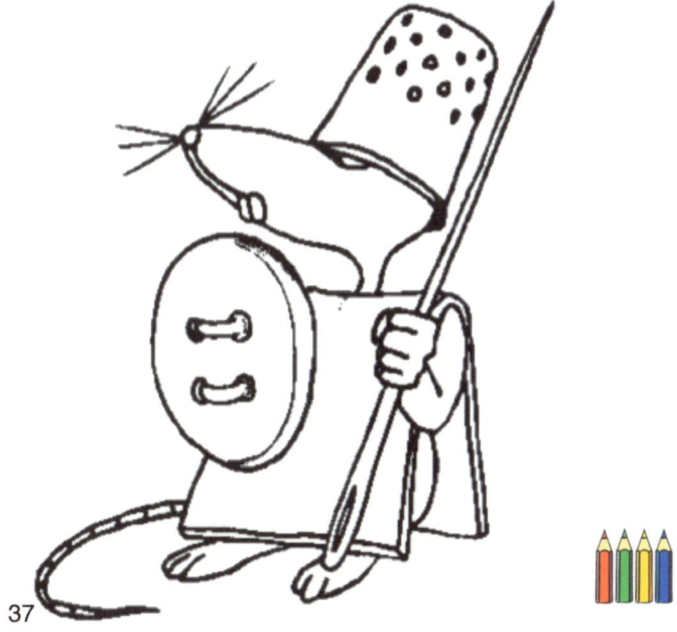

Lesson 9

1.

Warm Up

Partner clapping game:	Music and movement:

Partner clapping game:

1. Clap your hands 4 times.
2. Clap hands with your partner 4 times.
3. Repeat.

Make it harder:

1. 2 claps + 2 partner claps.
2. 1 clap + 1 partner clap.
3. Repeat!

Music and movement:

Danse Macabre

by Camille Saint-Saens

Listen for:

- Solo violin
- Orchestra (lots of instruments playing together)
- Short, spiky music
- Smooth, swaying music

Make up different movements for each character, listen and change movements when the music changes!

2.

Long Notes

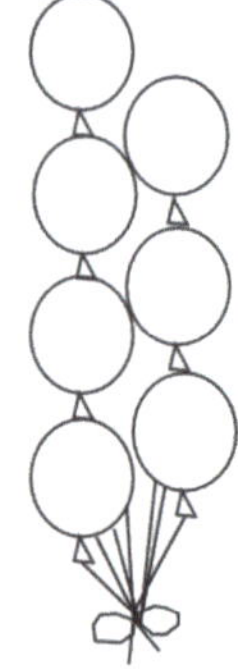

1. Hold up your LEFT hand.
2. Find a B on your instrument.
3. Play a B for 10 counts.
4. Play an A for 10 counts.
5. Play a G for 10 counts.

Listen carefully to your sound. Is it smooth and beautiful?

wiggles! 

While you blow a long note, lift your finger up and down to trill between A and B.

Now trill between G and A.

Can you trill between G and B? Which fingers have to move to do this?

3.

Revision

Can you name each of these?

B, A or G?

4.

Tongue

Start every note with the tip of your tongue.

Say:	"Too too too too"
Whisper:	"Too too too too"
Blow on your hand:	"Too too too too"
Blow on your instrument:	"Too too too too"

Can you tongue short and spiky STACCATO notes?

What about smooth LEGATO notes?

5.

Rhythm

Clap and say the rhythm names.

Choose which note to play.

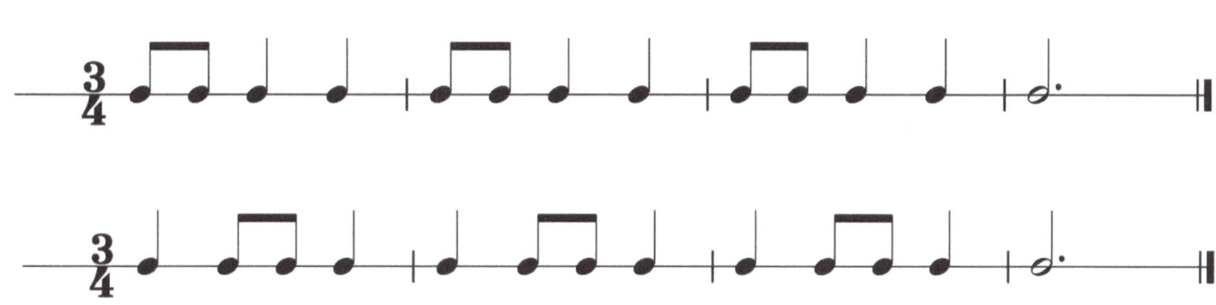

6.

New Song

Clap Sing Play

First: clap the rhythm
Next: sing the note names
Then: play it!

Waltz 

What do the two dots at the end mean?

7.

Listen - Clap - Sing

Listen carefully to a short melody.

Clap the rhythm back to your teacher.

Listen to the melody again.

Now sing it back!

Copycats!

Listen and then sing:

Doh re mi fah soh

Soh lah soh

Soh, fah mi re

Mi re doh

Soh mi soh

Soh fah mi re doh

Try some more Doh Re Mi patterns!

8.

Choose one person to be the soloist - everyone else is the orchestra.

•. The orchestra makes up a short theme to play together, for example:

B, B, A, B

• The soloist improvises a short solo.

• The orchestra responds with their theme.

Keep repeating, each time the soloist improvises a different solo and the orchestra answers with their theme.

9.

Have a go at writing the notes for the orchestra theme you composed.

Hint:

B goes around the middle line.

A sits in the second space.

G goes around the second line.

Supplementary material

Clap then play these rhythms on their own, as duets, or as a trio.

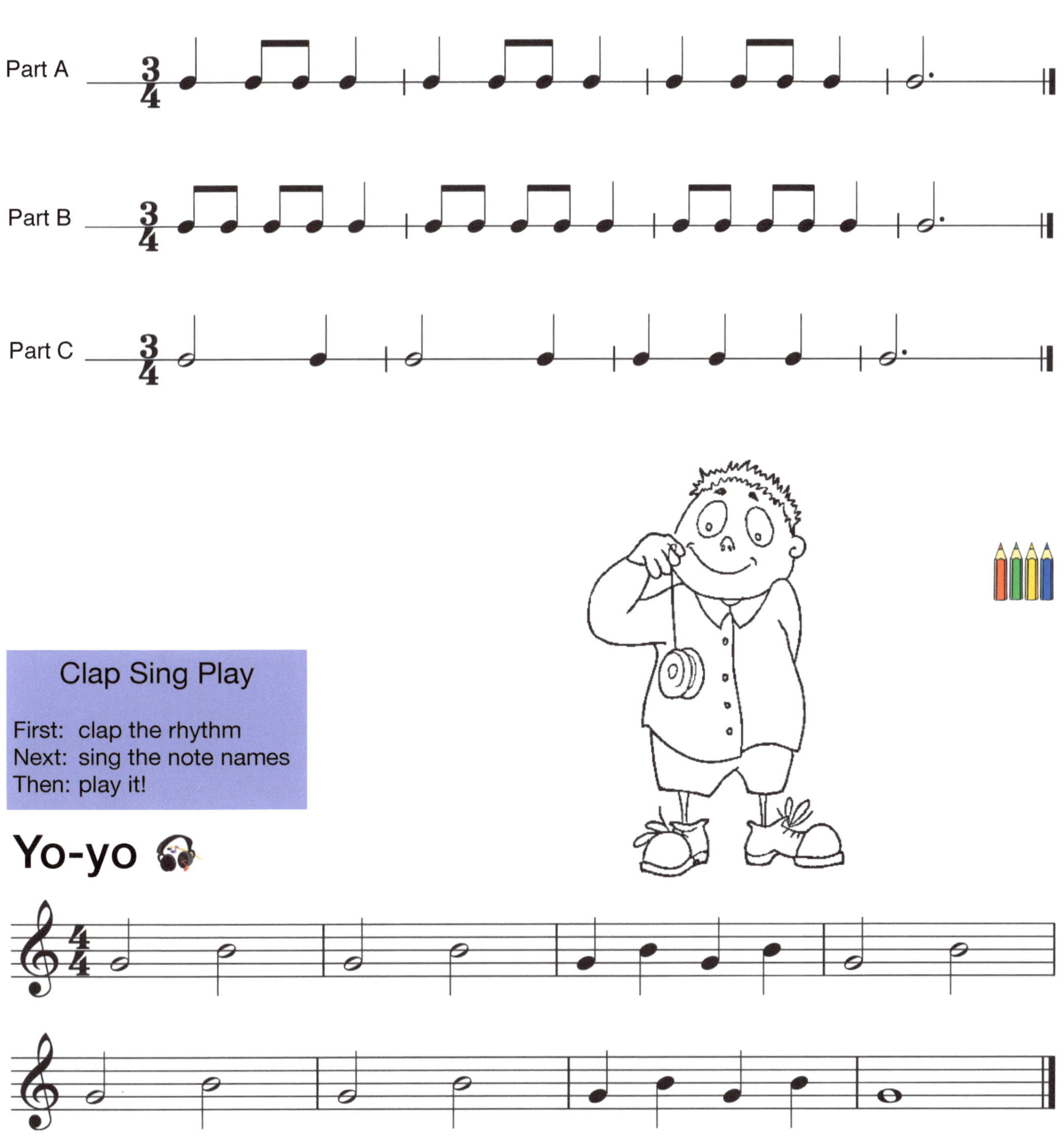

Go back and play some songs
from the previous lessons.

Lesson 10

1. Warm Up

Feet and Hands:

1. Keep the beat with your feet: **Ta Ta Ta Ta**

2. Clap one **Ti-ti**

Keep your feet going!

When you can do one Ti-ti, try clapping two or more in a row!

Music and movement:

Choose one of the songs you have done in a previous lesson to do again.

- *In the Hall of the Mountain King*
- *Intermezzo from Cavalliera Rusticana*
- *Dance of the Sugar Plum Fairy*
- *William Tell Overture*
- *Hedwig's Theme*
- *O Fortuna from Carmina Burana*
- *Swan Theme from Swan Lake*
- *Danse Macabre*

2. Long Notes

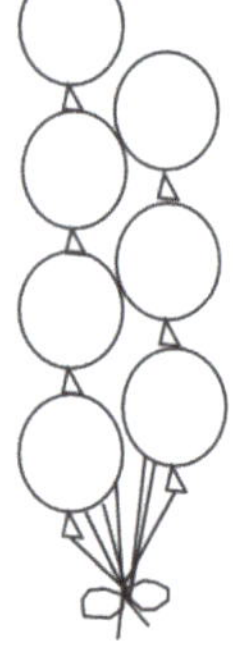

1. Hold up your LEFT hand.
2. Find a B on your instrument.
3. Play a B for 10 counts.
4. Play an A for 10 counts.
5. Play a G for 10 counts.

Listen carefully to your sound - is it smooth and beautiful?

wiggles! 

While you blow a long note, lift your finger up and down to trill between A and B.

Now trill between G and A.

Can you trill between G and B? Two fingers moving up and down together!

3. Revision

Can you name each of these?

B, A or G?

4.

Tongue

Start every note with the tip of your tongue.

Say:	"Too too too too"
Whisper:	"Too too too too"
Blow on your hand:	"Too too too too"
Blow on your instrument:	"Too too too too"

How many notes can you tongue clearly in one breath?

Write your answer here:

5.

Rhythm

Clap and say the rhythm names.

Choose which note to play

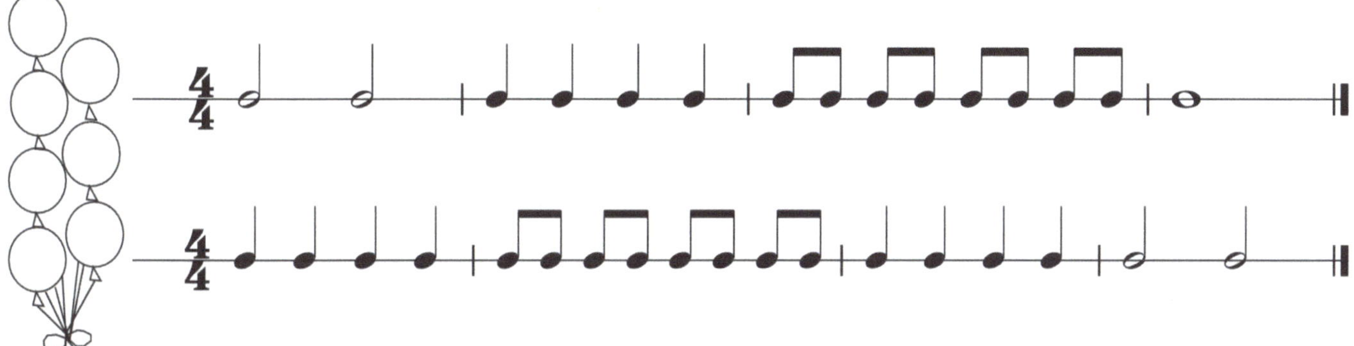

6.

New Song

Clap Sing Play

First: clap the rhythm
Next: sing the note names
Then: play it!

Shake Your Hips! 🎧

7.

Developing inner hearing*

1. Decide on a steady beat.

2. Think the beat internally, saying "1, 2, 3, 4" in your head.

3. Play a note on your chosen beat.

Make it harder: Everyone choose a different note to play on!

* See page 11.

Copycats!

Listen and then sing:

> Doh re mi fah soh
>
> Soh lah soh
>
> Soh, lah ti doh
>
> Doh ti lah
>
> Ti lah soh
>
> Soh fah mi re doh

Try some more Doh Re Mi patterns!

8.

Improvise!

Make up a short song called:

> "The Rabbit Hops, the Lion Roars"

You can use any sounds or notes to tell a musical story.

Supplementary material

Clap then play these rhythms on their own or as a duet.

Part A

Part B

Sparkle and Shine

Make up your own graphic notation to write the song you made up on the previous page. You can use lines, squiggles, circles, drawings - or anything you can think of to represent the sounds you made.

Can you think of three things you can do now, that you couldn't do when you first started this book? Write or draw them here:

1.

2.

3.

Stickers